ADOBE

ILLUSTRATOR

FOR BEGINNERS
2021

LEARN GRAPHIC DESIGN WITH
ILLUSTRATOR

Hector

Grant

COPYRIGHT

Printed in the United States of America

© 2021 by Hector Grant

RS Publishing House

USA | UK | CANADA

TABLE OF CONTENTS

INTRODUCTION

Adobe Illustrator is an application for creating beautiful and unique artworks. It is a vector graphics maker designed and developed by Adobe Inc in 1985. It is included as a part of the Adobe package, i.e., Adobe Creative cloud which includes Adobe Photoshop, Adobe Illustrator, Adobe InDesign, Adobe XD and more. This software is user friendly and supported by both WindowsOS and MacOS.

Furthermore, it is widely used by graphic designers for visual designs that combine shapes, text, and images. However, you can create different digital and printed artworks that include logos, icons, book covers, media post images, cartoons, business cards, and many more. Illustrator's most important use is its ability to create solid and quality artworks that are widely supported and used.

As a guide, this will walk you through the basics, which will ignite your ability to think creatively using Adobe Illustrator. You will get a simplified breakdown of utilizing this application by showing the various areas and tools on this platform. Hence, you understand how to use this software, creating colorful shapes and texts, sketching, shortcuts, tips and tricks, and many more… As you read through, it is advised that you practice along for easy and fast assimilation. So if you are ready, let us begin.

1.
GETTING STARTED

To everything, there is always somewhere it begins. In this part, we will go through the fundamentals of Adobe Illustrator. We will discuss the interface, things you need to know when creating a new document, saving your document, and in general, how to navigate within Illustrator.

THE INTERFACE

When you open Adobe Illustrator (of course, you must have installed it), what you see is called its interface. This is what you give commands and interact with to get your desired result. The interface contains three major segments; the top, the left-hand side, and the right-hand side.

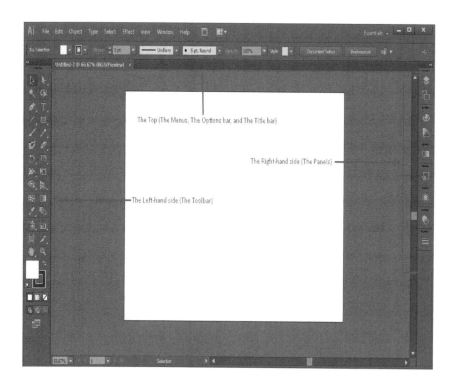

1. At the top is the Menus (File, Edit, Object, Type, Select, Effect, View, Window, and Help), the Options bar, and the Title bar.

THE TITLE BAR

THE OPTIONS BAR

The Menus allow you to do some specific functions like creating a new document, saving a document, and more. The Options bar allows you to modify your selected tool at a point in time. And the Title bar displays the title of the opened document(s).

2. On the left-hand side, we have the Toolbar. The Toolbar contains several tools that will help you work well and bring your imagination into reality. We have tools like the Pen tool for drawing, the shape tools, the Text tools, the Shape Builder tool, and many more.

3. And on the right-hand side are several panels for use; we have the Color panel (for choosing colors), the Swatches (for choosing preset colors), Layers panel, Stroke panel, and more. However, you can add more panels by clicking

the Window menu and selecting the panel you want.

When you open a panel, you minimize it by clicking the double-left arrow at the top right of such panel and click the x icon to close.

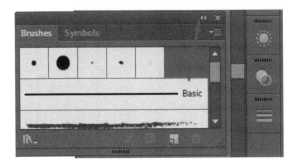

However, if you keep working with a specific panel, you can easily dock it by clicking and dragging such panel to the Panel bar.

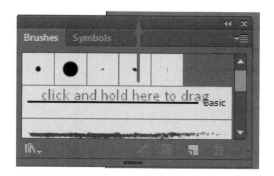

Now, you should be familiar with this fantastic software. So far, so good, we have discussed Illustrator's interface; the Menus, Options bar, Toolbar, and Panels. In the next topic, we will talk about creating a new document.

CREATING A NEW DOCUMENT

As soon as you open Adobe Illustrator, the next thing you most likely want to do is either open an existing document or create a new document. On a new document is where you work and can do all those fantastic things. So, let us create a new document.

You can create a new document through the File menu (File > New) or utilize the shortcut Ctrl or Command + N. Then, you get a pop-up window. This window allows you to make some settings to your new document.

Listed below are tips on the next thing to do:

➤ **Name:** Give your file a name; this will allow you to locate such a file quickly.

➤ **Profile:** This will allow you to choose based on the purpose you want to design. You can choose within Print, Web, Devices, Video and Film, Basic RGB, Flash Builder, and you can even browse for more. Mostly, you would be using Print and Web.

The Print option will change your color mode to CMYK (standard color for printing). If you are working on something like a T-shirt or a Poster, you need to work in that color profile. Web is the right selection when you are working on something for the Internet, a Logo or graphics for your website, for instance. Selecting Web will automatically change your color mode to RGB. However, you can always convert your color mode from RGB to CMYK and vice-versa.

➢ **Number of Artboards:** This option allows you to set the number of canvases or workspace you want. You also have the option to specify how they are arranged; you can make a Grid by Row, Grid by Column, Arrange by Row, and Arrange by Column. You can also choose Spacing and the number of columns you want, provided you have selected more than one artboard.

Two artboards

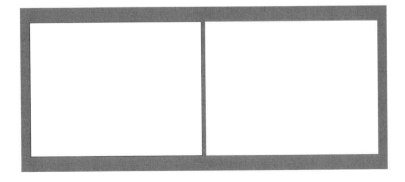

➢ **Size:** There are some preset sizes you can choose from, which are standard screen resolution sizes. But if you have a custom size you want to work with (creating a book cover, for instance), input the width and height values, and then choose the measurement you want (inches, millimeters, centimeters, etc.). You can also change the orientation (vertical or horizontal).

➢ **Bleed:** You can add bleed to your document at the top, bottom, left, and right. Bleed is a little bit of extra space you can add to your document, especially if you want something to be printed to the edge.

Now, as a beginner, input a name, set your Artboard to 2, make your width 12 inches and height 9 inches. Choose RGB as color mode, leave the rest, and click OK.

As soon as you do that, you have two different canvases, which are also your artboards. Your file's name is displayed at the top of the canvases, including RGB, to know its color mode.

Nevertheless, you can open an existing document through File > Open or press Ctrl or Command + O. You would be presented with a pop-up window, locate your file, and click Open.

You can also use File > Open Recent Files to open a file you just worked on.

CONVERTING YOUR COLOR MODE

As mentioned earlier, if you decide to change your color mode, go to Edit > Edit Colors > Convert to (any mode of your choice). For you to convert your color mode, you must have selected your artwork.

You can also change your current document color mode at File > Document Color Mode. The current model is ticked.

We have effectively discussed the basic way to create a new document and get started in Illustrator in a nutshell.

SAVING YOUR DOCUMENT

After creating an artwork, the next step is to save your work. Keeping your work in Illustrator is easy. You can save through File > Save or press Ctrl or Command + S. You also have more options in the File menu like Save As, Save a Copy, Save as Template, and Save for Web. The standard formats to save are the AI (standard illustrator format), EPS, or PDF (PDF is universal and can be opened everywhere you have a PDF reader).

However, you should use "File > Save as" to save in other formats different from the Illustrator's default format (AI). When saving a document, you get a pop-up window to give your file a name, choose a location, and choose a format. Once you complete those, click Save.

Then, you get another pop-up window. Here, you can choose to save your artwork in different versions of Illustrator. This works just the same way in Photoshop, where you can share your document based on your friends' software version. After choosing a version (the latest version is recommended anyway), do not worry about all other options. Click OK to save your file.

However, you might only be interested in saving your work as a picture with either JPG or PNG format. When your project is ready, all you have to do is go to File > Export... Then, you get a pop-up window to give your file a name, choose a location, and choose a format (for pictures, use JPG or PNG). Once you complete those, click Save.

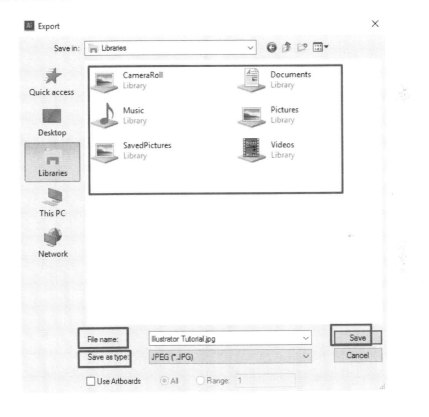

MANAGING
ARTBOARDS

To fully utilize your workspace, you have to learn how to manage your artboards. This involves adding, removing, and placing artboards.

TO ADD OR REMOVE AN ARTBOARD

Here is a quick way to add or remove an artboard. By your left, in the Toolbar, you have the Artboard tool (or press Shift + O on the keyboard to grab the tool), which you can use to move your artboards around.

You can add an artboard by clicking the new artboard icon at the Options bar.

Then, place the artboard anywhere you want. You shall notice green lines that guide you as you place the artboard; these are smart guides. You can turn on/off smart guides at View > Smart Guides.

However, to delete an artboard, grab the Artboard tool, click the artboard you would like to remove, and then click the Delete Artboard icon at the Options bar or press Delete on your keyboard.

Then, you can go ahead and rearrange other artboards. Click the Selection tool to restore to normalcy.

Adding more artboards is useful when you are creating a set of graphics on one file. Some instances are Business Cards, stickers, or multiple logos.

MOVING AROUND YOUR WORKSPACE

If at any point in time you want to move around your workspace freely, you can press H to grab the Hand tool, then click and drag your mouse to move around the document. This is effective when you are already zoomed in, and you want to see some details in your artwork.

Meanwhile, you can zoom in by grabbing the Zoom tool (you can press Z on your keyboard) and clicking on your screen. You then zoom out by pressing and holding Alt or Option on your keyboard and clicking on your screen. Once you are done, grab the Selection tool (always grab the Selection tool whenever you are done with a tool).

THE LAYERS PANEL

This is the Layers panel; you can have your artworks split into multiple layers. Using the Layers panel will help you manage your shapes, objects, texts, and images properly. Just like the Photoshop Layers panel, you can have different layers of the image. And as you proceed in this guide, you will understand precisely why the Layers panel is useful in graphics design.

To open the Layers panel, click on the icon at the Panel bar on your right-hand side. But if you cannot locate this icon, use Window > Layers to display the Layers panel.

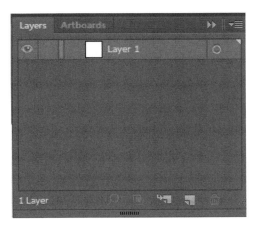

You can add more layers by clicking the new layer icon. You can turn on/off the visibility of a layer by clicking the eye icon. You can double-click the names to rename them. Also, you can delete a layer by clicking the Delete icon down below.

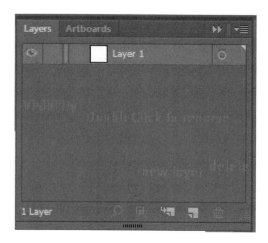

Now, you should be able to open a new document, navigate around your application, save a document, and know where your tools are situated. In the next part, we will discuss how to make use of the shape tools and draw.

2.

WORKING WITH SHAPES

Shapes are well used in graphics design and help to illustrate and communicate better to your viewer. Being good with shapes means you can edit and manipulate shapes into the beautiful thought of yours. In this part, we will talk about adding shapes, transforming your shapes, adding a color, manipulating your shapes, and more. For better learning, practice along.

ADDING SHAPES

It is time we start creating something. Allow us to begin with the Shape tools, which are all in the Toolbar. You can access the tools when you click and hold the Rectangle tool. Our basic Illustrator shapes are the Rectangle tool, Rounded Rectangle tool, Ellipse tool, Polygon tool, Star tool, and Flare tool. Some shapes are not present in the Shape tools; however, be assured that you will be able to form any shape of yours at the end of this part.

To draw a shape, grab the shape you would love to draw, and click and drag to draw. You can also draw a perfect shape by holding down the Shift key and then click and drag to constrain the proportion.

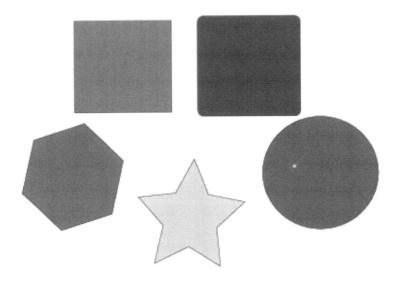

To delete a shape or anything, select the shape with the Selection tool, and press Delete on your keyboard.

TRANSFORMING YOUR SHAPE

When you open Illustrator, by default, you have the Selection tool selected. However, this is the most used tool because Illustrator is a vector program and made out of points, curves, and paths, your objects are scalable. You can quickly increase or decrease the size of your object.

Now, for you to change your object's size, select the object with the Selection tool. You should have eight handles around your selected object. Place your mouse on any of the handles, click and drag to see the effect.

Note: you can undo any changes you have made with Ctrl or Command + Z, and redo with Ctrl or Command + Shift + Z.

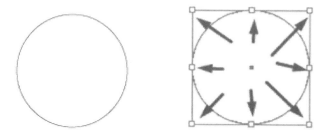

If you would love to transform your shape, you can switch to another selection tool known as the Direct Selection tool or press A on your keyboard.

As soon as you do that, select your object. Now we have four points instead of eight. As you hover your mouse over any of the points, you should see the smart guide come up that says, anchor. If you click on that point, you have more handles attached to that point. You can use these handles to transform your shape.

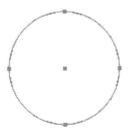

You can easily create this kind of shape by dragging the points. You can further adjust with the side handles. This now looks like an egg.

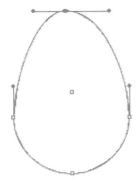

You can get a triangle from a rectangle by deleting a point out of the four points using the Direct Selection tool.

Click and press Delete on your keyboard

Then, grab the Pen tool, click on each of the two disjointed handles to draw a line to form the triangle.

Now, you can add color to your shape. See next page...

ADDING A COLOR

Now that you have your shape or object, it is time to make it beautiful. The swatches contain some preset colors you can quickly choose for your shape.

You can open the Swatches panel, which is by your right-hand side. If you do not have the Swatches panel, you can activate it through Window > Swatches. Now, form a shape, select your shape with the Selection tool, and then choose a color from the Swatches panel.

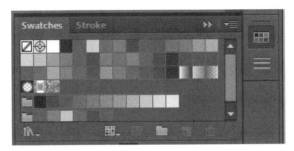

Now, let us form another shape and choose a color. There are always two colors to an object; you would notice that your shapes have a little outline around them. The color inside the shape is the Fill color, while the one outside is the Stroke color.

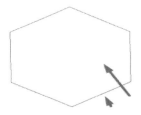

We have the Color Picker tool at the bottom of the Toolbar; the Color Picker contains the Fill color, Stroke color, and Swap Fill and Stroke (for swapping the Fill and Stroke color). You can add color to your Fill or Stroke by double-clicking the Fill or Stroke color option and then select your color.

However, you might want to use no color; this can be done by selecting either the Fill color or Stroke color and then click the no color icon (None). This will remove the Fill or Stroke color.

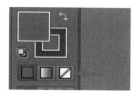

Let us place the smaller shape on the bigger one. Here, you would notice you cannot see through one of the shapes. Now, select the smaller shape and click the no color icon; you would now be able to see through it. Only the outline is left.

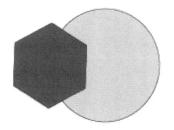 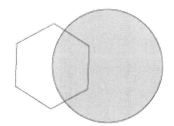

OBJECT ARRANGEMENT

In a situation where you want your shape like this and still want your color, but you want the bigger shape color to be in front. All you have to do is select the shape you want to be in the front, select Object > Arrange > Bring to front. Or right-click the object you want to be in the front, choose Arrange > Bring to front.

SEPARATING YOUR OBJECTS INTO DIFFERENT LAYERS

Another thing you can do to rearrange your shapes is to make use of the Layers panel. You can activate that through Window > Layer provided it is not already on your screen.

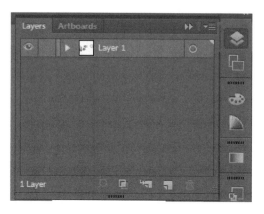

Presently, both of the shapes would be on the same layer. Now, select one of the shapes, and cut the shape by pressing Ctrl or Command + X. Then, create a new layer by clicking the new layer icon, and then press Ctrl or Command + V to paste the circle into the new layer. You should now see two different layers, and you can rename them if you like, as discussed in the previous part.

Now, be aware that layers are arranged according to how they appear. If you want a shape in the front, drag the shape layer up to the first. So, place the two shapes on each other, and then, on the Layers panel, click and hold to drag to switch the shapes layers position. This method would control the arrangement of your objects if you had them on the same layer.

CHANGING YOUR STROKE'S COLOR AND MAKING IT THICKER

Now, you know that the Stroke is the outline of your object, and you can also change its color and make it thicker.

Let us say you want to make a thicker stroke, select one of the shapes you drew earlier. Go to Window > Stroke or locate it at your Panel bar (its icon has three straight lines).

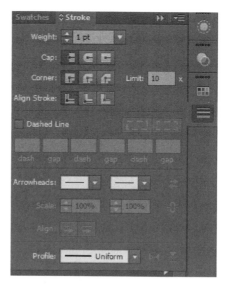

Once you click that, you would notice the option "Weight", and if you increase the weight value, your stroke becomes thicker. And the higher you go, the thicker it becomes. You can also make use of the drop-down menu and choose a size directly.

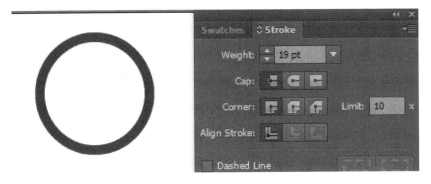

To change the stroke color, double-click the Stroke color picker at the Toolbar, and pick a color. You can also double-click the Fill color picker to change the Fill color as well.

Now, let us take a look at the effect of the Stroke on straight lines. Grab the Pen tool (located in the Toolbar), click once, hold down the Shift key and click the other end to form a straight line.

You might decide to change the ends of your line to something enticing; go to the Stroke panel again, you can change the weight, and then utilize the option called Cap and Corner. Also, play with the Dashed line, Arrowheads, and Profile options and observe closely the effects you get.

N/B: You can undo all the changes you have made using Ctrl or Command + Z to undo, or select all and delete.

SOME TIPS AND TRICKS

- As said earlier, with the Direct Selection tool, you can modify your shape by clicking and dragging the points to change the shape.
- You can click on a point with the Direct Selection tool and then delete to remove a part of your shape. After deleting a part of the shape, you need to close the shape by grabbing the Pen tool (or just press P), click on the first anchor point, and then click on the other anchor point to close the shape.
- You can make a copy of your shape by pressing Ctrl or Command + C, and then use Ctrl or Command + V to paste. You can also do this by pressing and holding the Alt key and just drag out the copied shape. You can also hold down the Alt + Shift keys at the same time to drag your new shape out in a line.
- To rotate your object, grab the Selection tool, place the cursor at one of the corners of the bounding box (your cursor should change into a curved arrow), and then click and drag. When you do this by holding the Shift key, it will rotate at an increment of 45°.

- You can join two different shapes into one solid shape by using the Shape Builder tool. All you have to do is select all the shapes by clicking the first shape, hold down the Shift key and click on the second shape. Then grab the Shape Builder tool. Now, click on one shape and drag it over to the other shape you want to join. Then, release your mouse and you should have your shapes joined as one. You can apply this same technique to more than two shapes.

EXERCISE

1. Draw a circle, make the Fill color red, make the Stroke color red, and set the Stroke thickness as 10. Draw another circle, make the fill color transparent, make the Stroke dashed line dots, and then make the Stroke color white. Now place the second circle on top of the first circle, and then bring the second circle to the front.
2. Draw a cylinder with the shape tools, and then merge the shapes used together as one.

3.

DRAWING AND COMBINING SHAPES

In this part, we will be building on what you have learned so far. You will learn how to use and become familiar with the Pen tool. It is vital to understand this tool's use if you want to do any illustration or vector-based work; we will be looking at the tips and tricks on using the Pen tool. We will cover the Pathfinder panel's use to combine shapes in unique ways, apply gradient fill, pick a color anywhere, and apply transparency and blending modes, which is also another significant Illustrator feature.

THE PEN TOOL

The Pen tool is used for drawing. It allows you to create curves or any kind of custom shape you want. This tool is also convenient when you are tracing something. If you have a photo, drawing, or illustration, you can scan it to Adobe Illustrator and then trace it to get the new object you want. You can draw anything you can imagine with this tool; however, you have to understand how it works to achieve that.

Now, open a new document with just one artboard. Grab the Pen tool or press P on your keyboard to select this tool. Click on your artboard, click on another end and hold, and then drag to create a curve. The idea is that, as you add points while still holding the mouse, you can drag around to create curves. When your cursor goes right, your curve goes left, and vice versa. To complete your drawing, click on the starting point. If you want to see the effect of what you are doing, ensure there is no color on the Fill, and make the Stroke color black.

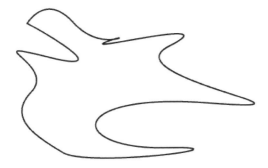

Whenever you are working with a pen tool, you also have handles that allow you to click and drag using the Direct Selection Tool, which is A on your keyboard. Those handles will help you modify your curves or points.

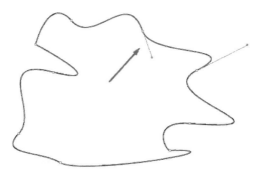

Also, be aware that there are more tools under the Pen tool. When you click and hold the Pen tool on your Toolbar, you have more tools like Add Anchor Point Tool, Delete Anchor Point Tool, and Convert Anchor Point Tool.

You can add a point at a particular spot if you want to manipulate and modify such area by grabbing the Add Anchor Point tool, and click on the spot on your path to add the point. You now have a new point with two new handles, which will allow you to modify your curve effectively.

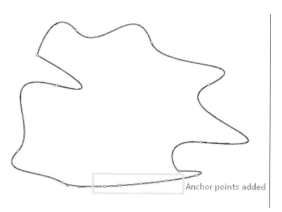

Anchor points added

You may also want to remove an anchor point. All you have to do is grab the Delete Anchor Point tool, and click on the point you wish to remove.

Now, go back to your normal Pen tool and keep drawing to master how the curves are formed. When you hold down the Alt key, you will notice your Pen tool changing to minus. This option lets you dictate the direction or length of the handle. You can make the line to become longer to influence the next point or make it short. At the end of each drawing, click the starting point to end the drawing.

Keep drawing, experiment with the handles, and form different shapes with it. However, you need a drawing tablet for the best result. You can also watch some videos on using the Pen tool on the Internet for more understanding if you are struggling using the tool.

COMBINING SHAPES

As discussed in the previous part, you can easily join two or more shapes together with the Shape Builder tool. All you have to do is place the shapes on each other, select the shapes you wish to combine, grab the Shape Builder tool, and then click and drag from a shape to the other.

However, there is another way you can join images together. This way is to use Pathfinder. This is amazingly useful to combine shapes; you can divide shapes, subtract shapes from each other, merge, and more. The Pathfinder panel is in Window > Pathfinder. It contains several methods to combine your shapes.

Now, let us take a look at each of the Shape Modes and Pathfinders. Create two different shapes and place one on the other. To join the two, grab the Selection tool, click and drag over the two shapes to select them.

Then, click on the first option called Unite. This would do the same thing as the Shape Builder tool, and you have your shapes merged into one.

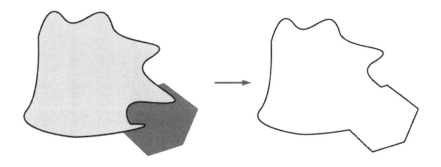

You can undo (Ctrl or Command + Z) this action and then use the next option. Select the two shapes and choose Minus Front on the Pathfinder panel. This will subtract the front shape out of the other shape.

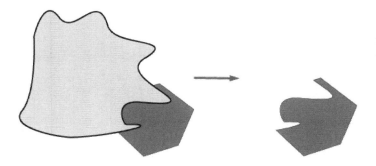

Now, make use of the rest and closely observe the effects. However, with an excellent creative mind, you can produce amazing logos using the Pathfinders. You might not see the usefulness now, but you will better understand how it works as we proceed.

LOCKING YOUR OBJECTS

You can always lock your objects after each design to avoid moving a part of the new shape by error. To lock your shape, select all of it (Ctrl or Command-A), and then click Object > Lock. You can also unlock through Object > Unlock to make changes in your new shape.

SELECTING ELEMENTS OF THE SAME COLOR

You can quickly select the same attributes like color, opacity, blending mode, stroke weight, and more. Now, draw a couple of shapes with at least two having the same color.

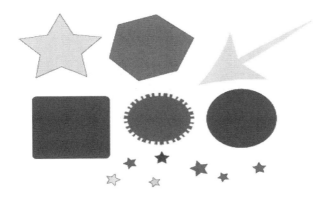

Now, you have different shapes with several colors. You can easily pick out shapes of the same color and change the color if you want. All you have to do is press A to grab your Selection tool, select one of the shapes, and then go to Select > Same > Fill color. Now, everything that is the same color as the shape selected would be highlighted. Then, you can proceed to change the Fill color provided that is your aim.

Besides, you can do more under Select > Same. You can choose everything with the same Appearance, Blending Mode, Fill & Stroke, Fill Color, Opacity, Stroke Color, Stroke Weight, and more.

Now, let us create more shapes using the Shape tools with different colors and strokes. Use the Select > Same, and then choose each of the options one after another to observe their effects. This will help you manipulate everything that has the same Fill color, Stroke color, or more.

One more thing, you can also select elements of the same color using the Magic Wand tool. Grab this tool or press Y on your keyboard, and click one of the objects. It then selects everything that is the same color. It works similarly. There is always a bunch of several ways to achieve the same thing in Adobe Illustrator. You just have to get to know as many of these options and features available to you as possible.

PICKING A COLOR ANYWHERE

You might want to reuse a particular color you have used before; the Eyedropper tool will allow you to do this. Let us say you would like to copy one of the colors you used earlier; select the shape you want the color, and then grab the Eyedropper tool or press I on your keyboard.

Then, click on the shape already having the color you want.

However, you can sample more colors anywhere, applying the same technique. Just create the new shape, grab the Eyedropper tool, click anywhere on your computer you want its color. Hence, the new shape is filled with the sampled color.

Moreover, you might be interested in knowing the hexadecimal value of a color. Grab the Eyedropper tool, sample the color you want on your screen, and then double-click the Fill color icon at the color picker. Then, copy the hexadecimal value.

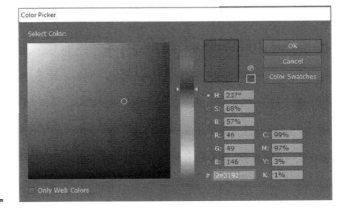

THE GRADIENT FILL

All this while, we have been using the Solid Fill color. Now, let us do something more attractive. You can make your artwork more beautiful by fading the color.

Let us create a Gradient Fill color. From the shape we created earlier, select one of them with the Selection Tool, or perhaps, you could create a new one. Now, click on the Gradient icon from the Color picker. This would give you a Gradient Fill, and also open the Gradient panel.

 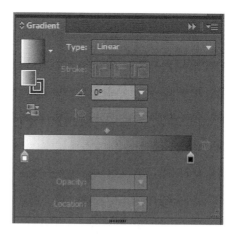

From the Gradient panel, choose a type. You can either choose Linear or Radial. You have the option to reverse the gradient, which will make it go the other way. You can also set a specific angle you want your gradient.

By default, the color you get is black and white. To add a different color to your gradient, double click the first Gradient slider on the Gradient panel.

Then, click the Swatches icon for more colors. Pick any color you want from the Swatches.

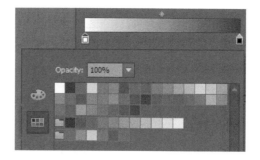

You can also click the Color icon for RGB sliders, which will allow you to modify your color as well, or you input a hexadecimal value if you have one.

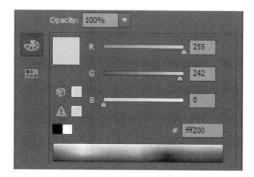

Now, follow the same steps and choose a color for the other slider.

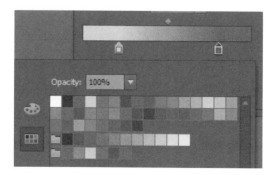

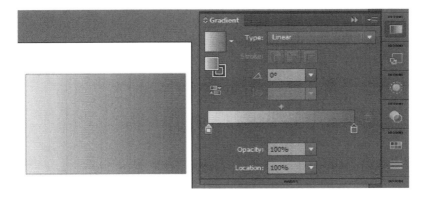

You can add as much color as you want as a Gradient; if you're going to add more than just two colors, double-click below the Gradient color box.

Then, double click on the slider, and then choose a new color, as discussed earlier. You can also play with the positions by sliding the sliders around.

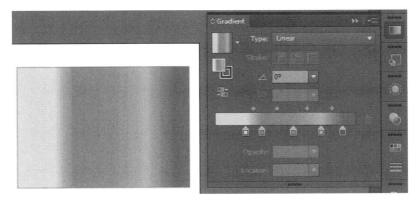

To delete a slider, undo the action. Or click the slider once, and then click the delete icon beside the Gradient slider.

So, that is the way you change a Solid Fill color to a Gradient.

TRANSPARENCY AND BLENDING MODES

Most times, while designing, you would need to place an object on another. And when you do this, you must find a way to make the objects blend well.

Let us use two different objects, for instance; you can create two new shapes or use the ones you have created earlier. Now, adjust the shapes sizes the way you would love them to be using the Selection tool (you can hold Alt + Shift, click and hold a corner, and drag to adjust or hold just Shift, click and hold a corner, and drag). You might also want to rearrange your shapes by using Object > Arrange as discussed earlier.

Now, click on the shape you would like to blend with the other. Open the Transparency panel through Window > Transparency. Reduce the Opacity to what fits best. Now, you have a transparent object that allows you to see what is beneath. This is a cool feature you can experiment with.

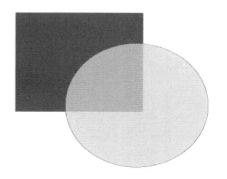 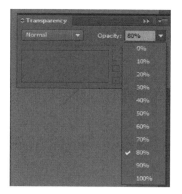

You can also change the blending mode. If you have ever used Photoshop, the blending modes in Illustrator should look similar to you. We have Normal, Darken, Multiply, Color Burn, Divide, and many more ways to blend your shapes.

Now, click one of the objects, and choose a blending mode. You can play with all these modes to know how they work and their effects while designing.

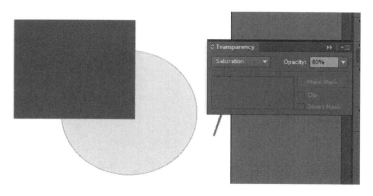

So, that is all for this part. I hope you now understand how these things work, using the Pen tool to create shapes, combining shapes, picking colors anywhere, applying the gradient, applying opacity, and blending modes. Please do not hesitate to go all over this part again if there is anything that seems unclear.

EXERCISE

Form different random shapes with the Pen tool. Combine these shapes with the Pathfinder panel. Blend these shapes and apply transparency where needed.

4.

WORKING WITH TEXT

TEXT

No matter how good you are at using shapes and objects to communicate to your audience, you just cannot do without using text. Text is more effective and complimentary. Nevertheless, in this part, we will be covering different things you can do in Illustrator with texts. We will also discuss how to convert your text into outlines and modify texts into something interesting creatively.

It is okay if you still want to use the old document, or create a new document as shown previously for this part. To start, grab your Text tool from the Toolbar. Click anywhere on your artboard, and type "WORKING WITH TEXT".

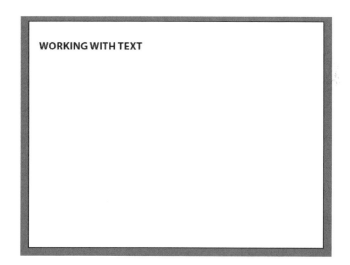

WORKING WITH TEXT

TEXT SIZE

After typing something, there is always a need to adjust the text size to fit correctly. It might be to make the text either larger or smaller. All you need to do is grab the Selection tool, press and hold the Shift key, and then drag one of the four corners to enlarge the text.

WORKING WITH TEXT

Like the shapes, you can also press and hold Alt + Shift simultaneously and then drag one of the four corners.

Another way to change your text size is to press Ctrl or Command + Shift + (or).

You can also change your font size at the Options bar.

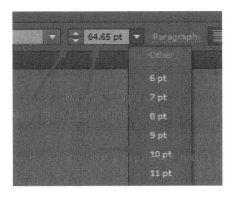

You can click one point at a time. You can type manually or use the drop-down menu to pick a value.

These are the ways you can adjust the size of your text.

TEXT FONT

There are several fonts to use in Illustrator. You can access these fonts at the Options bar. But before you can see the Font icon, you must have selected your text with the Selection tool. Click on the Font icon and choose a font.

If you would like to preview the font you are selecting, click on the Character panel's Character icon.

Click the Font icon and scroll till you get what you want. You can also get a preview of the font your cursor is placed on.

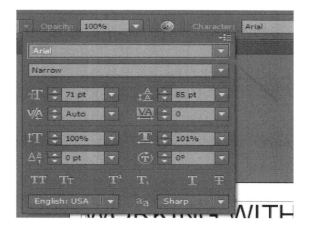

Below is the Font icon in the Font Style icon, which contains Narrow, Regular, Italics, Bold, and more, depending on the font you have selected. You can go ahead and manipulate your text using the adjustment settings in the Character panel.

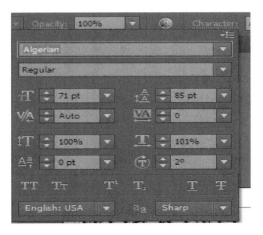

You can also make your text either upper case or lower case, set superscript or subscript, underline, and strikethrough.

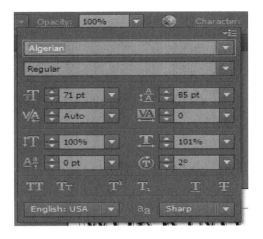

ADJUSTING TEXT SPACING

When it comes to graphics design, you can easily tell if someone is good at it how well text is used to communicate. Your text must not stress your audience to denote, and you can achieve this by using the right amount of spacing in your text.

If you want to correct the spacing in your text (you want to add or remove space), grab your Text tool or press T, and then click and drag from your text's beginning to the end.

click and drag to the end of the text

Then, press Alt or Option + the right arrow on your keyboard to add more space and Alt or Option + the left arrow to reduce the space. You can also adjust the line spacing when your text is on two or more lines. To do this, highlight the text, and then press Alt or Option + the upper or lower arrow key. Or use the "Set the leading" icon on your Character panel to adjust line spacing.

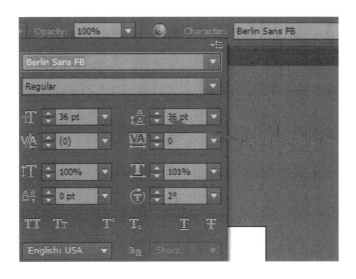

Yourcan → You can
rearrange

When you are done, you can grab the Selection tool.

COMPARING FONTS

Sometimes you might not be sure of the font to use; however, you can easily compare two or more fonts and then decide. Let us compare other fonts with the selected one above. Now, press and hold Alt or Option + Shift, then drag out a copy of your text with the

Selection tool. Click the copied text and choose any type of font you like. This simple method will allow you to compare fonts easily.

WORKING WITH TEXT

WORKING WITH TEXT

FORMATTING

You can rearrange your text in a specific manner. You can align to the left, center, right, and justify. To do this, select your text, click on the Paragraph icon at the Options bar or go to Window > Paragraph, and select the alignment you prefer.

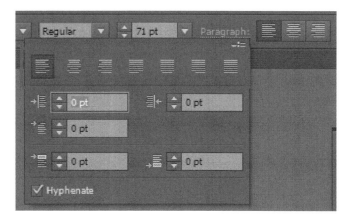

This is usually used when your texts are much; two or more lines. It helps place your words in a particular order.

Left

You can rearrange your text in a specific manner. You can align to the left, center, right, and justify. To do this, select your text, click on the Paragraph icon at the Options bar or go to Window > Paragraph, and select the alignment you prefer.

Center

You can rearrange your text in a specific manner. You can align to the left, center, right, and justify. To do this, select your text, click on the Paragraph icon at the Options bar or go to Window > Paragraph, and select the alignment you prefer.

Right

You can rearrange your text in a specific manner. You can align to the left, center, right, and justify. To do this, select your text, click on the Paragraph icon at the Options bar or go to Window > Paragraph, and select the alignment you prefer.

Justify

You can rearrange your text in a specific manner. You can align to the left, center, right, and justify. To do this, select your text, click on the Paragraph icon at the Options bar or go to Window > Paragraph, and select the alignment you prefer.

MODIFYING YOUR TEXT

Let us assume you have found a font you like, and you still wish to modify some of the individual letters. To do this, you have to convert such text to outlines.

Now, create a copy of the text as described earlier (press and hold Alt or Option, then drag it out) so that you do not lose the original text should something goes wrong. Click the copied text you wish to modify, then go to Type > Create outlines (Ctrl or Command + Shift + O). Once you do that, you would notice several points around your letters.

Several points

Now, grab the Direct Selection tool, click on a point, and drag it out. You can press and hold Shift and then click on the points to select multiple points if you want. This goes well and amazing when doing logo design to create a wordmark logo.

WORKING WITH TEXT

UNGROUPING TEXT

You can also ungroup the text (Object > Ungroup), then rearrange or move each letter around for better positioning depending on what you want. To ungroup: select the text with the Selection tool and go to Object > Ungroup. Then, click on each letter and drag it out. You can resize each letter the usual way, depending on the logo you are working on. You have to broaden your thinking cap and be more creative to do amazing things with texts.

WARPING TEXT

Again, you can modify your text by giving it a curve. Sometimes you see logos with curves, and it looks incredible. The easy way to do this is by clicking on the text (selecting the text with the Selection tool) and then going to Object > Envelope Distort > Make with

Warp. Then, you get a pop-up panel; check the preview box to see the effect of the changes you make.

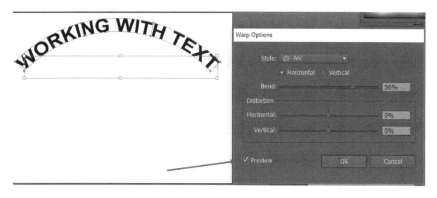

You have the Style drop-down menu to pick from. You can choose where you want the arc to face, whether horizontally or vertically. There are sliders you can play with to determine how much bend you want. When you are done manipulating the text, you click OK.

In a situation where you would still like to expand your text by creating outlines as described earlier, go to Object > Expand. Then, tick Object and Fill, and click OK. Now you should have all your points back, which you can manipulate. You can also ungroup the text if you want to form something or leave it grouped if not.

**CHANGING THE
COLOR OF YOUR TEXT**

No doubt, colors will make your text feel amazing.
However, you should be aware that your text also has
two colors, just like the shapes. There is both the Fill
and Stroke; the Fill fills the inner part of your text, and
the Stroke is the outline color of your text.

Stroke Fill

You can easily apply any of these by selecting your text
and then choose to apply either Fill or Stroke at the
color picker. However, you might just want to apply
both depending on what you want and how it blends
with your project.

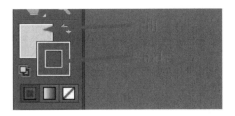

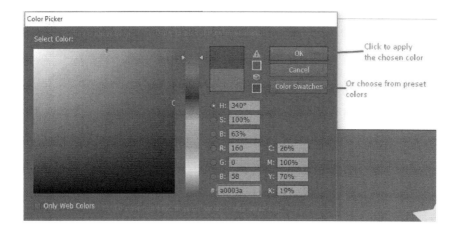

You can also use the Fill and Stroke swatches at the Options bar to pick a color for your text.

MAKING YOUR STROKE THICKER

You can also increase the thickness of your text's stroke to bring out the chosen color for stroke. This enhances the way your text looks. All you have to do is select the text, then locate the Stroke icon at the Options bar. Increase the stroke one point at a time and stop when satisfied with the result.

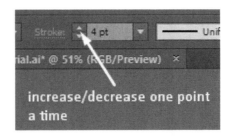

increase/decrease one point a time

WORKING WITH TEXT

Fill = Red   Stroke = Yellow

5.

THE ART TOOLS

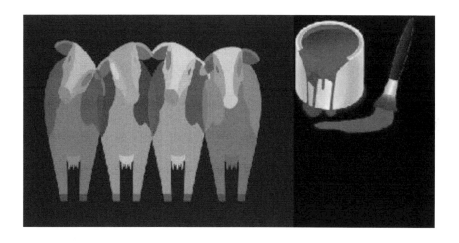

In this part, we will discuss the use of some of the art tools in Illustrator. We will be looking at how to trace a photograph, use the inbuilt preset brushes, create custom art brushes, and load art brushes you downloaded from the Internet. We will also be looking at some other useful tools like the Arc, Spiral, Rectangular Grid, and Polar Grid tools that can be used to create interesting design flourishes. We will then discuss how to use the Eraser, Scissors, and Knife tools in Illustrator.

Let us build on the use of the Pen tool. Here, we will trace a photograph and turn the photograph into vector art.

Now, open the image you would love to trace using File > Open. Before we step in, for a start, use an image with lesser details. As you get better, you can then work on more complex images.

Now, lock the image you just opened at the Layers panel (Window > Layers).

Create a new layer and draw a big rectangular shape on your screen to fill the new layer. Ensure the Fill is white.

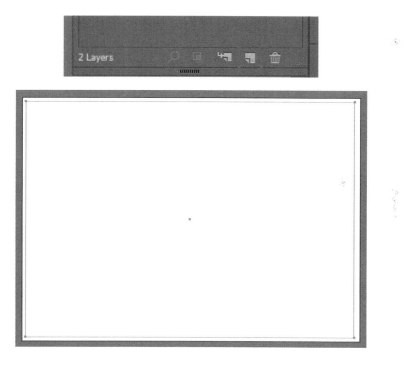

Now, open the Transparency panel and reduce the new white layer's opacity to about 30%. That would allow you to see clearly what you are about to draw.

Then, lock this layer as well.

Now, grab your Pen Tool, make sure your Stroke is black and Fill is no color. Then, you can begin to trace the outside part of the object and gradually move to the inside part (click and click to make points as you trace the object). Utilize the Zoom tool for a better view where needed. However, this might be time-consuming and somehow hard, depending on how detailed your image is.

Whenever you get to an endpoint, grab the Selection tool, then grab the Pen tool to start another point.

To check what you have done so far, hide the image layer by clicking the eye icon on it to reveal your vector shape. Click again to reveal the image layer and continue.

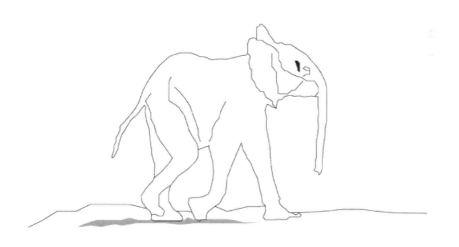

Once you are done tracing your image, you might be interested in making it colorful, which you can do with the color picker tool. But be aware that the Fill color would only work on closed shapes you formed while tracing, and not lines. However, you can apply Stroke color to both closed shapes and lines.

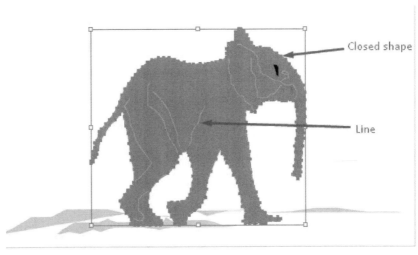

Now, you can save your document or export it as a picture for your personal use.

Brushes are not only used for painting but also drawing if well utilized. You can sketch and draw with this tool. However, there are several kinds of brushes, and all you have to do is select one according to your need. Some are scattered. Some are used for arts, while some are for drawing patterns. Now, let us play and explore the use of Brushes in Illustrator.

Now, create a new document. Grab the Paint Brush tool from the Toolbar. On the canvas, click and hold, then drag on your screen to draw different random lines. You can change your paint color just the normal way we have discussed (select a color for your Fill and Stroke at the Options bar or use the color picker on your Toolbar).

One of the cool things about this tool is that you can create your custom art brushes or download one from the Internet. However, you can display the Brushes panel to view all your brushes through Window > Brushes.

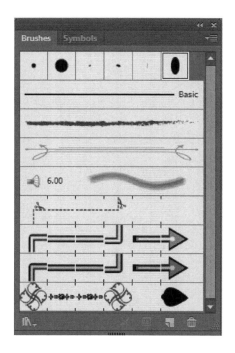

On this panel, click the menu icon at the upper right and select Open Brush Library. You should see some preset brushes in Illustrator; you choose one according to your need, and however, select Artistic brushes > Artistic_Paintbrush for learning. Artistic_Paintbrush panel will then pop out. You can scroll down the panel to get more of the brushes for amazing results. Click one of the brushes, then draw on your canvas to apply.

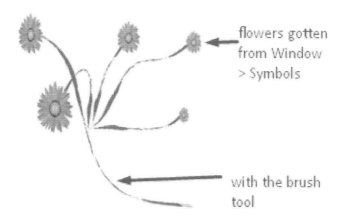

flowers gotten from Window > Symbols

with the brush tool

Play and explore with other brushes and think of the things you can create with them.

CREATING YOUR BRUSH

If you would like to use some other brushes aside from the inbuilt ones, you could create one for yourself. To do this, grab the Rectangle tool and draw a rectangle just as it is below, and not your regular rectangle. Then, make the Fill and Stroke black.

Now, you can design the two ends as you wish. Zoom in (grab the Zoom tool and drag on the area to enlarge) the right end and grab your Ellipse tool. At the right end of the rectangle, press and hold Shift to draw a perfect small circle.

Then, slide the circle inward, select both shapes, and use the Pathfinder tool as thought earlier to unite the objects.

 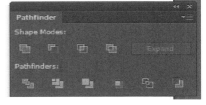

You can give the other end another cool shape if you like. You can modify it using the Direct Selection tool. When you are done, select the new shape you formed, and then click on the Brushes panel menu.

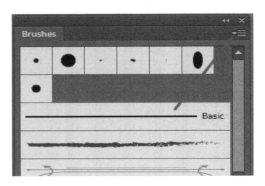

Choose New Brush, and you get a pop-up panel showing the types of brush. Choose Art Brush (choose a brush according to the category you want to put it), and click OK. You get another pop-up window, give your brush a name, tick Scale proportionately, and leave other settings. Click OK to add your brush to the list of brushes.

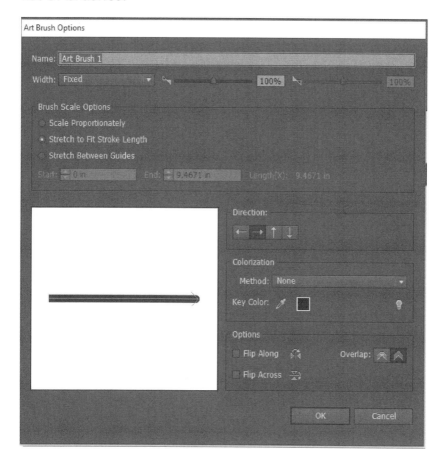

Now, you should have your new brush in the Brushes panel. Grab your Paintbrush tool, select your new custom brush, and then click and drag to draw.

You can create any shape and turn it into a brush for your use in Illustrator.

MODIFYING YOUR PAINT

Let us say you want to remove a couple of pixels from your paint; you can do this by expanding the paint. Select the paint with your Selection tool, go to Object > Expand Appearance. Grab the Direct Selection tool (press A on the keyboard), and this will allow you to select some of the individual points. You can decide to modify your paint (click and drag around to modify). You can also delete some part of the shape by selecting the part with the Direct Selection tool, and then press Delete on your keyboard.

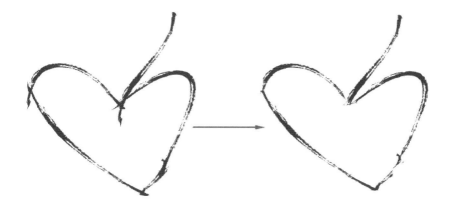

INSTALLING BRUSHES

If you had downloaded some brushes on the Internet, you could quickly install them by locating the Illustrator folder through the File Explorer (Windows user) or Finder (Mac users). In your Programs Files (Windows) or Applications (Mac), go to Adobe > Adobe Illustrator > Preset > Brushes, and then paste the brushes here.

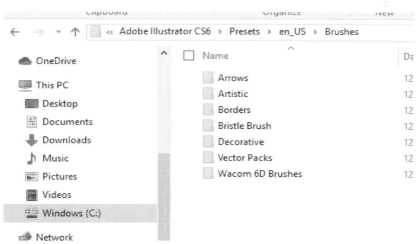

Once you do this, you should look at your newly installed brushes up in the brush library. Just open the Brushes panel, click the Brushes panel menu, and then select Open Brush Library.

OTHER ART TOOLS

Some of the other cool art tools are the Arc, Spiral, Rectangular Grid, Polar Grid, Pencil, Smooth, Blob Brush, Eraser, Scissors, and Knife tools. They are as important as other tools, and as you become better at Illustrator, you have more reasons to utilize these tools. Now, let us see how they can help you while designing.

THE ARC TOOL

Now, click and hold the Line Segment tool and then choose the Arc tool.

Click and drag to draw an arc. You can apply a brush by choosing one from the Brushes panel; however, you can choose your newly created brush. Then, you get a nice curve looking arc, which you can further enhance. Press and hold Alt or Option + Shift and drag to draw a perfect arc. You can also rotate, flip around, add color, and manipulate as you want.

THE SPIRAL TOOL

Like every other tool, grab the Spiral tool within the Line Segment tool and draw.

For a perfect shape, press and hold Shift as you draw. You can also make it more spiral by pressing and holding Alt or Option + Shift as you drag.

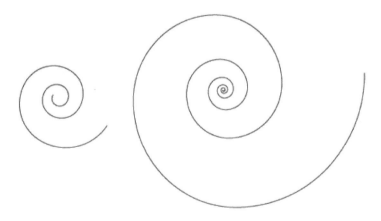

Now, apply a custom brush to your spiral shape for a beautiful nice effect (select the Spiral shape with the Selection Tool, then choose a brush type from the Brushes panel). You can decrease or increase the stroke for a better look, as the case may be. You can also go ahead and add color to get a beautiful look.

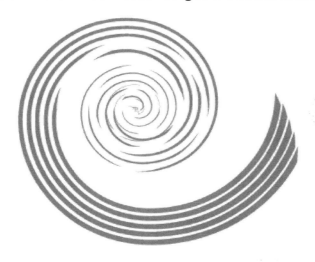

You can even merge with other shapes using the Pathfinder panel to create nice logos. Or just add them as nice flourishes and decorative elements to an illustration or design.

THE RECTANGULAR GRID TOOL

We also have the Rectangular Grid tool, which helps in creating a pattern-like object. Grab this tool by clicking and holding the Line Segment tool, then draw.

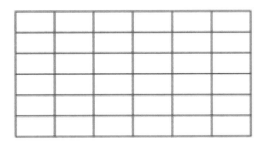

THE POLAR GRID TOOL

You can utilize this when you are doing an interface design. Grab this tool by clicking and holding the Line Segment tool, then draw.

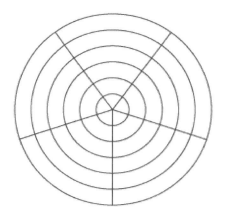

You can apply a custom brush to your Polar Grid shape for a beautiful nice effect (select the shape with the Selection Tool, then choose a brush type from the Brushes panel). You can decrease or increase the stroke for a better look, as the case may be. You can also go ahead and add colors for a beautiful look.

THE PENCIL AND SMOOTH TOOLS

The Pencil tool also works similarly to the Brush tool. However, with the Pencil tool, you can smoothen out your path when applying the Smooth tool. The Smooth tool can be found when you click and hold the Pencil tool on the Toolbar.

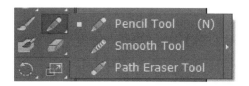

When you draw with the Pencil tool, you can complement your drawing with colors and custom brushes in the Brushes panel.

THE BLOB BRUSH, ERASER, SCISSORS, AND KNIFE TOOLS

The Blob Brush tool is just a thicker form of the Brush tool. You can use this just precisely the way you would use your brushes.

You have some unwanted marks on your project that you want to erase or cut out; the Eraser tool would do the job correctly.

Aside from the Eraser tool, other useful tools are the Scissors and Knife tools. The Scissors tool only allows you to cut objects along a path, and then you can separate the shape with the Direct Selection tool. However, the Scissors tool would not work on a Fill. This tool is located underneath the Eraser tool.

With the Knife tool, you can easily slice your shape into two or more parts. Once you do that, you need to ungroup (Object > Ungroup) the shape to separate the parts.

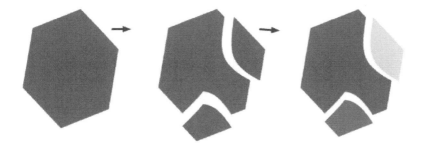

EXERCISES

1. Create this below by combining a square with a spiral. You are free to work with any color of your choice.

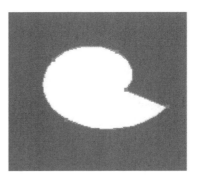

2. Create a beautiful effect similar to this using the Polar Grid tool, Direct Selection tool, colors, and Brushes panel.

3. Create this below using a circle, the Knife tool, and colors.

6.

TRANSFORMING OBJECTS

In this part, we will be combining most of the things we covered in the previous parts. We will discuss how to use the Blend and Envelope Distort options to transform your objects into something unique. We will also discuss the use of the Gradient and Mesh tools and how to create 3D text.

THE BLEND
AND ENVELOPE DISTORT TOOLS

With these tools, you can create some cool effects which can be used as a part of your project. You can use these effects as backgrounds, logos, and more. Now, let us take a look at the things we can do with these two tools.

THE BLEND TOOL

The first thing you should do here is to create a new document. Then, grab the Pen tool, set your Fill to no color, and Stroke to black.

By now, you should have experimented with the Pen tool and be good at it. You should use the anchor points to create the kind of shapes and curves you want. And be rest assured, the more you do it, the better you become. Now, draw something like the shape below.

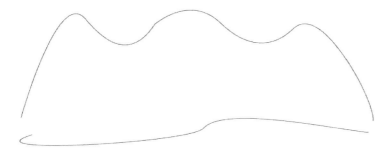

In the course of drawing, sometimes you might need to rotate your image. To rotate an object, select the object, and go to Object > Transform > Rotate. You get a pop-up, check the Preview icon to see the changes you make, and then use the Angle to rotate your object.

Right now, our shape contains just two different curves. Select the top curve and increase the stroke weight to become thicker. You can adjust your stroke weight with the Stroke panel (Window > Stroke), then set the value around 5pt.

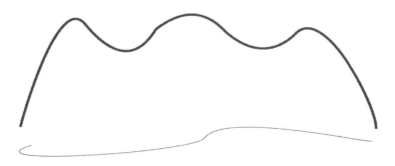

Now, select both lines with the Selection Tool, then go to Object > Blend > Blend Options. You get a pop-up, choose Specified steps as spacing, input 10 as the value, and press OK.

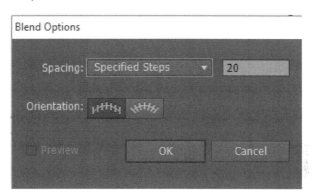

Again, go to Object > Blend > Make or press Ctrl or Command + Alt or Option + B. Then, you get cool wavy lines going from thicker to thinner.

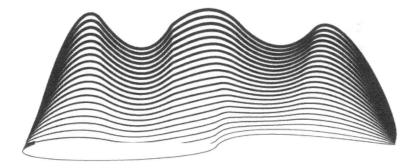

You can even go-ahead to increase/decrease the number of lines by Object > Blend > Blend Options. You get a pop-up, mark the preview box, change the number, and then click OK. Now, you should have more/fewer lines in between the object, as the case may be. Once you are okay with the lines, you can either leave it like that or keep working on it.

You may also want to change the object into points for easy altering by using Object > Expand just as we have done previously. Then, you alter with the Direct Selection tool.

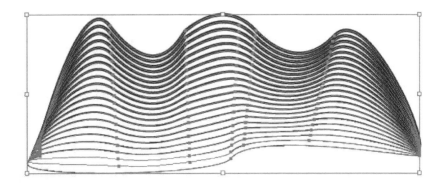

Besides, you can add both Fill and Stroke colors.

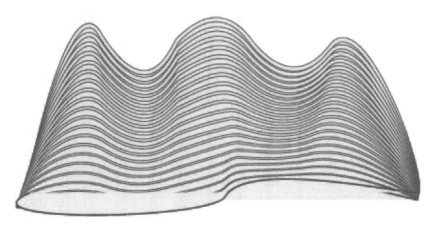

THE ENVELOPE DISTORT TOOL

Now, let us make a copy of the new shape. Perhaps, you may need to readjust the size before making a copy. Press and hold the Shift key, and then drag inwards from the bottom right corner. To make a copy, press and hold the Alt or Option key + Shift key, and then drag out the copied object.

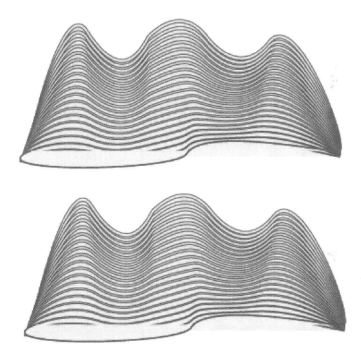

Now, select the copied shape and go to Object > Envelope Distort > Make with Warp (you can also apply this option to shapes and not just text). Now, tick the preview box, and choose a style. There are several kinds of styles you can use here. Play with the sliders. You can get more impressive results by exploring this.

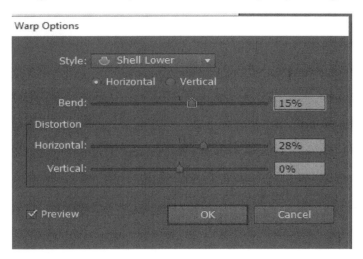

Using Make with Mesh

With our new shape selected this time around, let us choose something more different. Again, go to Object > Envelope Distort, instead of Make with Warp, choose Make with Mesh.

Make with Mesh allows you to take your shape to another level and determine how many rows and columns you want to have for easy transformation. For instance, choose 5 rows and 5 columns. Now, you have the mesh on your object.

Grab the Direct Selection tool, double-click, and drag any of those points to modify your shape. You can also select multiple points by pressing and holding Shift as you click on the points. This process gives you more control to distort your shape. Play with this and come up with something unique.

All these will help you create background elements for your arts.

CREATING PATTERNS

You can create a pattern with the shape you have drawn.

To do this, select your object, go to Object > Pattern > Make. Then, you get a pop-up panel and a message saying that your new pattern would be added to your Swatches panel for use.

From the Pattern panel, you can give your pattern a name and choose a tile type. Then, click on Done around the Title bar.

Now, your pattern has been added to the Swatches. You can quickly draw any shape and make the pattern your Fill.

Now, do this. Make your Fill no color, and your Stroke the pattern (click the Stroke icon once, go to Window > Swatches, then select the pattern. However, you must increase your Stroke weight to see the effect of this pattern.

This is a three-dimensional form of objects. This process helps create the illusion of depth in an object. Here, we will look at the ways you can achieve that with both shapes and texts.

THE MESH TOOL

This is a fantastic tool for creating a 3D-like object. It is simple and easy to use, and the more you play with it, the better you become.

Now, grab the Ellipse tool, press and hold the Shift key, and then draw out a perfect circle. Then, click on the Mesh tool.

Click the middle of the circle to add a point. Now, click on the other sides of the circle to add more points, as shown below.

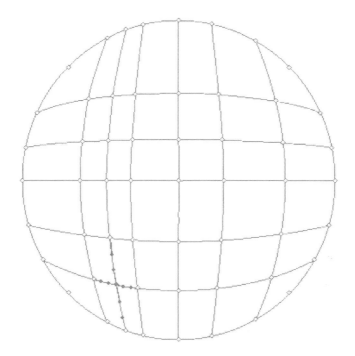

Then, select the entire circle with your Selection tool, and choose a fill color.

The fantastic thing about this is that you can select those points with your Direct Selection tool, go back to your Fill color, and choose another color. You could hold down the Shift key to select multiple points if you needed to use the same color. Keep playing with the color, and let us see what you would come out with.

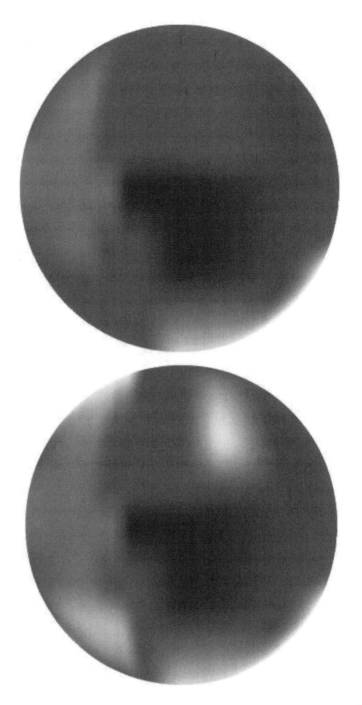

This way, you can create a more realistic looking object by adding more points and changing colors.

3D TEXT

Doing 3D with text is simple and easy to achieve. As it was thought earlier, with the Text tool, type something. If needed, adjust the font and size of your text. Then, make a copy of your text by pressing and holding Alt, click and hold your text, then drag out a copy.

3D TEXT

3D TEXT

Now, select the copied text and convert it to outlines using Type > Create Outlines (this will convert your text into a shape). Now, go to Object > Envelope Distort > Make with Warp, then you can choose a suitable style for this. You might also want to adjust the text slightly with the warp sliders; once done, click OK.

Now, go to Effect > 3D > Extrude & Bevel. You get a pop-up box, tick the preview option at the bottom left corner of the box for a live view of the changes you make.

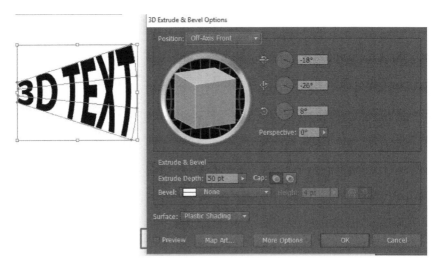

Now, click on More Options, then choose Custom under Shading color.

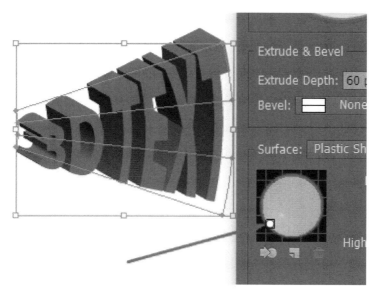

You now have a small color icon by your right, double click on this icon for more colors. You can change the direction of light in your text with this box below.

Also, you can change the Extrude Depth and Bevel. From 50, you can make it 70, then observe the effect on your text. If you are not okay with it, change the figure.

You also have this box option that allows you to rotate your text the way you want. Once you are done adjusting things, press OK.

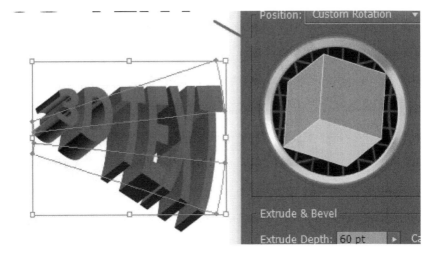

You might be interested in going further; you can decide to bright your text up or add more colors. Now, select your object with the Selection tool, and go to Object > Expand Appearance. That will allow you to control your text by breaking it up into shapes and points.

Now, you can grab the Direct Selection tool, press and hold Shift, click on each face of the letters in the text. Click on the Fill icon, and choose a brighter or another color. Play with this, and let us see what you will come up with.

Please be aware that it is not compulsory to use the Object > Envelope Distort > Make with Warp option before you can make a 3D text. All you need is to type your words, then proceed to Effect > 3D > Extrude & Bevel. Then, you can utilize Object > Expand Appearance to add a font color. Practice and explore this.

Furthermore, if you are interested in adding a shadow effect to your text, make a copy of your text with the

Alt method. Then, select your text, and make the Fill color grey.

You can now reduce the Opacity of the shadow text to like 30%, as discussed previously. Then, go to Object > Transform > Reflect. You get a pop-up, set your Angle at 180°, and click OK.

Now, with the Selection tool, drag the shadow text inwards and readjust the shadow text size if need be. Now, you have your shadow effect on the 3D text.

WHAT NEXT?

So far, we have been able to touch every fundamental aspect of graphic design using Adobe Illustrator. What remains is practicing and exploring. Now, *how do you explore?*

When it comes to technology, always put it at the back of your mind that "I must keep learning". Now, be prepared to create fresh artworks from already designed arts/graphics. These could be logos, illustrations, book covers, social media post graphics, banners, business cards, and other graphic designs. Now, be prepared to do the following:

➢ Design logos. Get several free logo samples from the Internet. Form each of these logos one after another all by yourself in Adobe Illustrator. Then, with your creative mind, think of a product or service, and create a brand logo.

➢ Design book covers. Look around you for book covers, and create as many as possible book covers you can. However, you must be aware that measurement is required to design book covers. We have different book sizes ranging from 5 * 8, 6 * 9, 8 * 11, and more. First, you have to generate a book cover size on the Internet to know what size you need to make your document. Then, with your creative mind, think of different book topics, and create corresponding book covers for them.

➤ Design business cards. Get free samples of business cards from the Internet, and create the same. Then, with your creative mind, think of a product or service, and make a business card.

➤ Trace photographs. Get a couple of pictures on your computer for tracing. Apply the things you have learned in this guide about image tracing, then come up with beautiful artworks.

Nevertheless, those are only a few of what you can do in Illustrator. Prepare to challenge yourself to create any graphical material (physical or virtual) you see.

THE END

Thank you for reading this book. I hoped it was practical and useful to you.

Below are some other books you may have interest in;

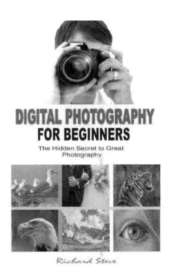

Printed in Great Britain
by Amazon